THE WORLD OF MYTHOLOGY:

MIDDLE EASTERN MYTHOLOGY

BY JIM OLLHOFF

VISIT US AT
WWW.ABDOPUBLISHING.COM

Published by ABDO Publishing Company, 8000 West 78th Street, Suite 310, Edina, MN 55439. Copyright ©2012 by Abdo Consulting Group, Inc. International copyrights reserved in all countries. No part of this book may be reproduced in any form without written permission from the publisher. ABDO & Daughters™ is a trademark and logo of ABDO Publishing Company.

Printed in the United States of America, North Mankato, Minnesota.
022011
092011

 PRINTED ON RECYCLED PAPER

Editor: John Hamilton
Graphic Design: Sue Hamilton
Cover Design: Neil Klinepier
Cover Photo: Gonzalo Ordóñez
Interior Photos and Illustrations: Alamy-pgs 12, 15, 17, 18, 22, 23, 24 (right), 27, & 29 (bottom); Balage Balogh-pg 16; Caitlin Crowley-pg 19; CIA-pg 7 (Middle East map); Corbis-pgs 8 & 20; Getty Images-pg 9; Glow Images-pgs 5 & 24 (left); Granger Collection-pgs 6, 14, 25 & 26; Inspyretash-pg 13; iStockphoto-border image; Mary Harrsch-pg 29 (top); Norman Einstein-pg 7 (Fertile Crescent Map); Thinkstock-pgs 11, 21, & 28

Library of Congress Cataloging-in-Publication Data

Ollhoff, Jim, 1959-
  Middle Eastern Mythology / Jim Ollhoff.
     pages cm. -- (The World of Mythology)
  ISBN 978-1-61714-725-8
  1. Mythology, Middle Eastern--Juvenile literature. I. Title.
  BL1060.O45 2011
  398.20939'4--dc22

                          2010042977

CONTENTS

THE MIGHTY MYTH

Ancient people liked to sit around the fire in the evening and tell each other stories. The stories were told to their children, and the children grew up and told those same stories to their children. "Myth" is from the Greek word *mythos*, which means "story." A myth is just a story that helps us make sense of ourselves and the world.

Today, we still like to tell stories. We like to sit around school lunchrooms or business offices and recount last night's television shows. We like to talk about good movies we've seen. We like to tell stories of exciting things that have happened to us.

Myths are stories that give us meaning, whether they are factually true or not. The Santa Claus myth (not factually true) tells us something about the importance of the holiday. The myth of the Pilgrims coming to America (factually true) tells us something about independence, adventure, and the sacrifice it took to start a new country. The myth of George Washington chopping down the cherry tree (probably not factually true) illustrates the importance of honesty.

One of civilization's first great stories was about a man-god named Gilgamesh. The "Epic of Gilgamesh" is a story about his many adventures, but mostly it's a story about how he went from being a selfish, evil king, to a humane, wise ruler.

We're not that much different from ancient peoples. We still love a good story.

Above: The Epic of Gilgamesh is one of civilizations's first great stories. Gilgamesh was a man-god who had many adventures. In one story, he met the goddess Ishtar, who fancied Gilgamesh, but he was not interested in her. She sent a bull to kill him, but Gilgamesh slew the bull.

THE MIDDLE EAST

The Middle East, sometimes called Western Asia, is a large area of land between Europe and Asia. Its boundary is often considered to be from modern-day Egypt in the southwest, to Turkey in the north, to Iran in the east. Historians sometimes use the term "Fertile Crescent" to describe a smaller part of the Middle East. The Fertile Crescent is the land surrounding the Tigris and Euphrates Rivers in present-day Iraq and western Iran, and down through modern-day Israel, Syria, Lebanon, Jordan, and northern Egypt's Nile River Valley.

The Fertile Crescent was once a place where the soil was rich for growing crops. Today, much of the Fertile Crescent is no longer fertile, and has been taken over by desert. However, many civilizations grew up in the land of the Fertile Crescent. This area suffered under constant fighting for centuries. Cities and countries warred against each other. Empires rose and fell. Roving tribes moved in and out, often bringing warfare with them.

Right: The Middle East area known as the "Fertile Crescent" once was an excellent place for growing crops.

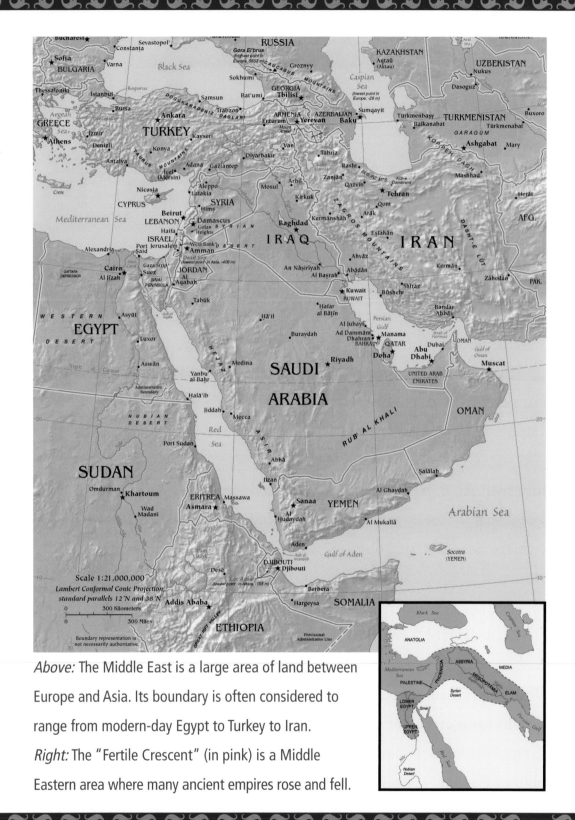

Above: The Middle East is a large area of land between Europe and Asia. Its boundary is often considered to range from modern-day Egypt to Turkey to Iran.

Right: The "Fertile Crescent" (in pink) is a Middle Eastern area where many ancient empires rose and fell.

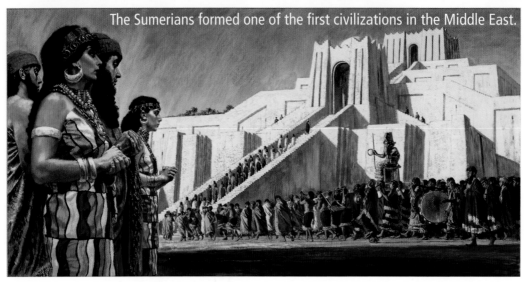
The Sumerians formed one of the first civilizations in the Middle East.

The Sumerians formed one of the first civilizations in the area, probably starting around 3000 BC. They began as a number of city-states in the area called Mesopotamia, between the Tigris and Euphrates Rivers. Within a few hundred years, a people called the Akkadians came to power. They defeated the Sumerians around 2340 BC. After several hundred years of occasional fighting, the Babylonians rose to power, with their capital in Babylon. Assyrians became the dominant force around 1170 BC. The Chaldeans came to power in about 612 BC, and within a few hundred years, the Greeks moved in.

In the land of Canaan, along the eastern side of the Mediterranean Sea, smaller governments were the norm. The Canaanites, Hebrews, Philistines, Amorites, Phoenicians, and a wide variety of small tribes fought for dominance and survival. But when the massive armies of Egypt and Mesopotamia fought each other, they traveled through the land of Canaan, often ransacking the land as they went.

Above: Akkadians came to power by defeating the Sumerians around 2340 BC. There were many wars in the Middle East in ancient times.

The Soul of Middle Eastern Mythology

Even though the rulers of Mesopotamia changed often, the myths and gods of the area were much more stable. When one nation conquered another nation, they often merged the conquered gods into their own mythology. Sometimes, it's impossible to tell from which nation a myth started because they used and reused each other's myths. The stories were told, revised, added to, and retold. Gods were renamed. Old stories were connected with new stories. Old gods were reinvented.

The climate of the Middle East was often harsh. Dangerously hot summers, very cold winters, and disastrous flooding were common. Likewise, the gods and goddesses of the Middle East were also often harsh and cruel.

The Middle East often suffered from droughts. When it didn't rain, the crops wouldn't grow. Then there would be no food to eat, leaving the possibility of mass starvation. So, the gods of agriculture and rain, called fertility gods, were very important to the people. The people had many rituals and practices that they believed would force the gods to make it rain.

Above: The Middle East often suffers droughts, so the gods of agriculture and rain were very important to people.

BABYLONIAN CREATION

The story of creation from Babylon is called the "Enuma Elish." These are the first two words of the creation story. This story is often called the "Babylonian Creation," but parts of it are found in earlier cultures, as far back as the Sumerians.

Before there was an Earth, or stars, or people, there was the god Apsu and the goddess Tiamat. Apsu and Tiamat had several children, and those children had children, and so on. The great-grandson of Apsu and Tiamat was Ea, the good and wise Earth god.

Above: The Babylonian Creation story was written on seven clay tablets.

All those children, however, made a terrible amount of noise. They stayed up late and made far too much racket. They kept old Apsu awake all night, and so he decided to kill all of them.

Above: Tiamat was the Babylonian goddess of the sea.

Ea, the wise Earth god, found out about Apsu's evil plan, and used his power to protect the other gods and to kill Apsu. Tiamat, however, was angry that Ea killed her husband, Apsu. So, she and her new husband Kingu planned to kill Ea using snake monsters and scorpion-men. Ea found out about this, and he and his wife gave birth to Marduk. Marduk agreed to fight Tiamat and Kingu, but in return he demanded to become the supreme god if he won the battle.

Marduk killed Tiamat and Kingu. He cut Tiamat in two, making one half of her body the sky, and the other half of her body the Earth. Marduk then made human beings out of the blood of Kingu.

All the other gods and goddesses were so grateful to Marduk that they made him the supreme leader of all the gods, and then built the city of Babylon for him.

Above: The Babylonian god Marduk defeats and slaughters the monster and sea deity Tiamat, out of whose remains he would fashion the Earth and sky.

Above: Marduk became the supreme leader of all the gods.

GILGAMESH, KING OF URUK

One of the oldest stories in human civilization is the story of Gilgamesh. It is more than 4,000 years old. Gilgamesh was

Above: Uruk, a massive city along the Euphrates River.

the legendary King of Uruk, a massive city along the Euphrates River. Gilgamesh was part god and part man. The city of Uruk actually existed, and was discovered by archeologists in the year 1849.

Gilgamesh was a selfish king who didn't care about his subjects. He spent his time abusing the people of Uruk. Things got so bad that the people of Uruk prayed to Anu, the god of the sky, to help them.

There was a creature who lived in the desert named Enkidu. Enkidu was partly a man, but mostly an animal. He was so wild that he even talked with the other animals. Slowly, he had been learning how to live as a human. The god Anu sent Enkidu to fight Gilgamesh.

Above: An Assyrian sculpture of Gilgamesh, King of Uruk, holding a lion.

Gilgamesh and Enkidu fought each other for a long time, wrestling and punching. Gilgamesh won the fight, but just barely. The two realized that they were almost equal, so they became friends.

Above: Gilgamesh rejects the goddess Ishtar, and she becomes angry with him. She sends the Bull of Heaven to destroy the city of Uruk.

The goddess Ishtar was angry with Gilgamesh, so she sent a giant monster called the Great Bull of Heaven to destroy the city of Uruk. Gilgamesh and Enkidu fought the Bull of Heaven, and they killed it. However, Enkidu died after the fight. Gilgamesh was terribly sad and grieved a long time.

Gilgamesh buried his friend. Because of Enkidu's death, Gilgamesh realized that he might die someday. He went on a great quest, looking for the secret of immortality. Gilgamesh wanted to live forever, and went on a journey to find immortal gods. After a long time, and many adventures, Gilgamesh came close to finding the secret of immortality, but never could get his hands on it. He went home to Uruk, thinking he had failed. But when he saw the great city of Uruk, he realized that the city where he reigned was a wonderful city. He realized that he had succeeded in his quest for immortality, because the story of his deeds would survive long after his death.

Gilgamesh was right—the story of his mythical deeds has indeed survived to this day!

Above: Gilgamesh and Enkidu face off against the Great Bull of Heaven.

CANAANITE ORIGIN OF THE SEASONS

In the land of Egypt, rain was less important for crops because the Nile River always flowed and gave water. But in the land of Canaan, rain meant crops would survive, and no rain meant the crops would die—and the people might starve. So, in the land of Canaan, rain gods were very important.

Baal was the Canaanite storm god who brought rain to the crops. He was the chief of all the gods. In one story, Mot, the evil god of the underworld, invited Baal to come down to visit. In another version of the story, the evil Mot threatened to turn the whole Earth into a desert unless Baal surrendered. In both versions, Mot kills Baal. With Baal dead, rain no longer fell on the crops, and everything dried up.

Left: Baal, the Canaanite storm god and the chief of all the gods.

Baal's wife Ashtoreth sought revenge on Mot. She went to the underworld and killed him with a sickle. Then she burned him, ground him up, and scattered him over the fields, just like a farmer does with grain.

Baal was revived and returned to bring rain, but was killed by Mot every winter. This cycle replays every year, and so the seasons were created.

Above: Ashtoreth scattered Mot over the fields, just as a farmer does with grain.

MESOPOTAMIAN GODS AND GODDESSES

Mesopotamia is the land between the Tigris and Euphrates Rivers, where Kuwait and Iraq exist today. It was the land of the Sumerians, Akkadians, Babylonians, Assyrians, Persians, and many others. The civilizations shared many myths and borrowed stories from each other.

Ashur is often pictured with the sun.

Ashur: He was one of the most powerful of the Assyrian gods. He was the god of Earth, air, and sun. In some of the myths, he was the husband of Ishtar. He is often pictured with the sun, which reflects his position as the sun god.

Above: The goddess Ishtar seeks her husband Tammuz in the underworld, but is kept captive there by evil forces.

Ishtar: A popular Babylonian goddess, Ishtar is sometimes the goddess of love, sometimes the goddess of agriculture, and sometimes the goddess of war. She seemed to always be getting herself into trouble.

Tammuz: The husband of Ishtar, Tammuz was the god of vegetation and spring. In the beginning of summer each year, the heat made growing crops too difficult. People believed that this was because Tammuz died and went to the underworld. There was a weeklong ritual called "weeping for Tammuz," where people grieved for Tammuz and the lack of crops.

Lilith: Probably of Sumerian origin, Lilith was a terrifying goddess of death. She stole babies and turned them into monsters. Her myths survived into Roman times, where she was believed to be a vampire-like spirit.

Mithra: An ancient sun god, Mithra drove his chariot across the sky each day. Later, he became a god of truth, wisdom, and warfare. He is sometimes pictured with a terrible wild boar that would attack his enemies. His myths survived until Roman times, when he became especially popular among the Roman military.

Adapa: According to Babylonian mythology, Adapa was the first man. He was the son of Ea, the wise Earth god. Despite being a human, Adapa had great strength and wisdom. He invented language and gave it to humanity. One day, when he was out fishing, a strong wind blew and overturned his boat. Adapa was so angry that he tore off the wings of the wind. Adapa was then called to heaven to explain his actions. Ea told him to humbly apologize, and to not eat any of the food there, because it was poisonous. As it turned out, the gods of heaven were so impressed with Adapa's humble apology that they offered him the food of immortality instead of the poison food. Adapa didn't realize this, so he refused to eat any of the food. So, since then, humans have remained mortal.

CANAANITE GODS AND GODDESSES

Canaan is the land along the eastern Mediterranean Sea, where Israel, Syria, and Jordan exist today. Some of the myths and gods were shared with the civilizations in Mesopotamia. Canaanite gods were used in many different ways by many different cultures. It is sometimes hard to identify who they were or what they did.

Baal was the god of thunder, storms, and rain.

Baal: One of the most important gods was Baal, the god of thunder, storms, and rain. Because rain was so important, Baal was widely worshipped. In some areas, Baal was believed to be the god of the sun, and was feared. It seems that many ancient cultures in the area had differing beliefs and myths concerning Baal.

Ashtoreth was the wife of Baal.

Ashtoreth: She was a goddess who had many different myths, from many different cultures. Depending on the civilization, she was known as Asherdu, Astart, or Athtart. Sometimes she shared the same stories as another goddess, Anat or Anath. She may have been known as Ishtar in Mesopotamia. Ashtoreth was the wife of Baal, and was sometimes known as the goddess of love, and sometimes as the goddess of war. Some historians think she was the source of Aphrodite, who was worshipped by the Greeks.

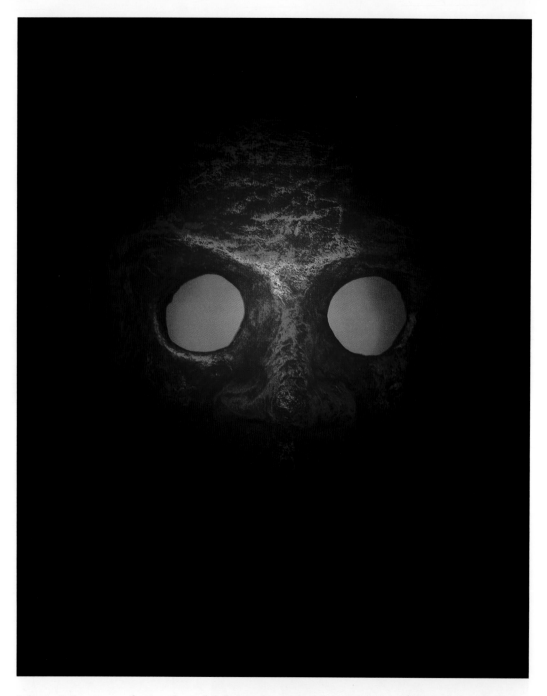

Mot: Mot was the evil god of death and the underworld. When there was a drought or crop failure, people blamed Mot. He was sometimes seen as the archenemy of Baal.

El: The father of all the gods was El. He was the creator of everything, and chief among the gods, but he was impersonal and remote. He was often pictured wearing bullhorns, which are a symbol of strength.

Tarhun: Also known as Tarhunt, he was a god of the Hittites, a people who lived in northern Canaan. A god of the sky and storms, he was often pictured carrying a thunderbolt. He carried an ax or some other weapon, and was often accompanied by a sacred bull. His wife was Arinna, the sun goddess. One popular myth tells the story of how Tarhun killed the evil dragon Illuyanka.

GLOSSARY

BABYLON

An ancient capital city in Mesopotamia on the Euphrates River. Myths say that Babylon was built by the gods for the supreme god, Marduk.

CANAAN

The land along the eastern Mediterranean Sea, where Israel, Syria, and Jordan exist today.

DROUGHT

An extended period of time when rain does not fall.

ENUMA ELISH

An ancient creation story written in poem format by the people of Babylonia. The poem is named after its first two words: Enuma Elish.

EUPHRATES RIVER

Originating in Turkey, the Euphrates River flows into the Persian Gulf. It forms the southern and western side of the area called Mesopotamia.

FERTILE CRESCENT

The crescent-shaped swath of land from Mesopotamia to Canaan to the Nile River Valley. It was once a very fertile land.

IMMORTALITY

The ability to never die.

MARDUK

The supreme god from the Babylonian creation story. Marduk killed the goddess Tiamat and cut her in two, making one half of her body the sky, and the other half of her body the Earth. Marduk then made human beings out of the blood of Kingu, Tiamat's second husband.

MESOPOTAMIA

The land between and near the Tigris and Euphrates Rivers, where Kuwait and Iraq exist today.

MIDDLE EAST

Sometimes called Western Asia, it is the land from Turkey to Egypt, and from countries bordering the eastern Mediterranean Sea to Iran.

NILE RIVER

The world's longest river, at about 4,160 miles (6,695 km), which flows through central and eastern Egypt.

TIGRIS RIVER

Originating in Turkey, the Tigris River flows into the Persian Gulf. It forms the northern and eastern side of the area called Mesopotamia.

INDEX